Sew Stylish
COLORING BOOK

JESSICA MAZURKIEWICZ

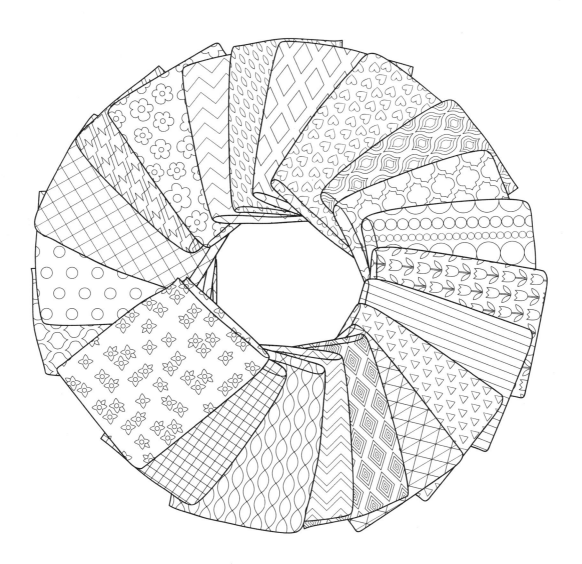

DOVER PUBLICATIONS, INC.
MINEOLA, NEW YORK

The pleasures and rewards of sewing are many, and this delightful coloring book provides an array of illustrations of this ever-popular craft. You'll find charming images of sewing machines; patterned fabrics; a variety of buttons; dress forms; needles and thread, as well as scissors and pinking shears; and the sewing projects themselves, including hand-sewn toys designed for pet cats and dogs! Wise words for sewers are scattered throughout the pages. Just select the colors of your choice as you enjoy the artistic possibilities of this very special collection— plus, the perforated, unbacked plates make displaying your work easy!

Bibliographical Note

Sew Stylish Coloring Book is a new work, first published by Dover Publications, Inc., in 2018.

International Standard Book Number
ISBN-13: 978-0-486-82915-9
ISBN-10: 0-486-82915-4

Manufactured in the United States by LSC Communications
82915401   2018
www.doverpublications.com

Happiness is HOMEMADE

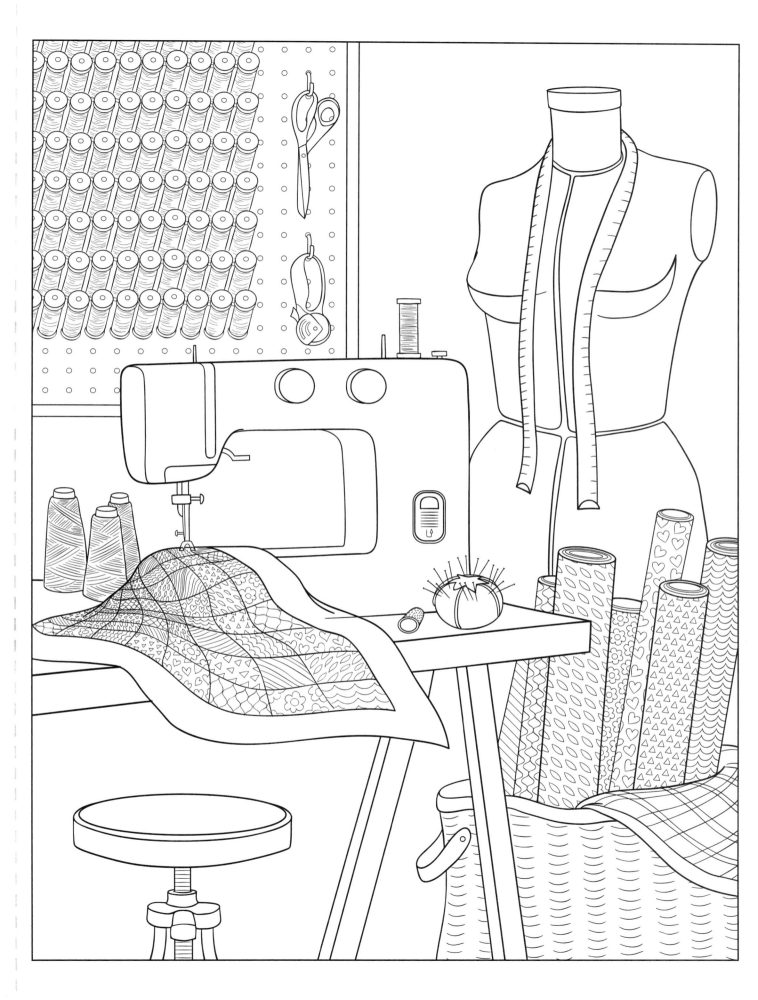

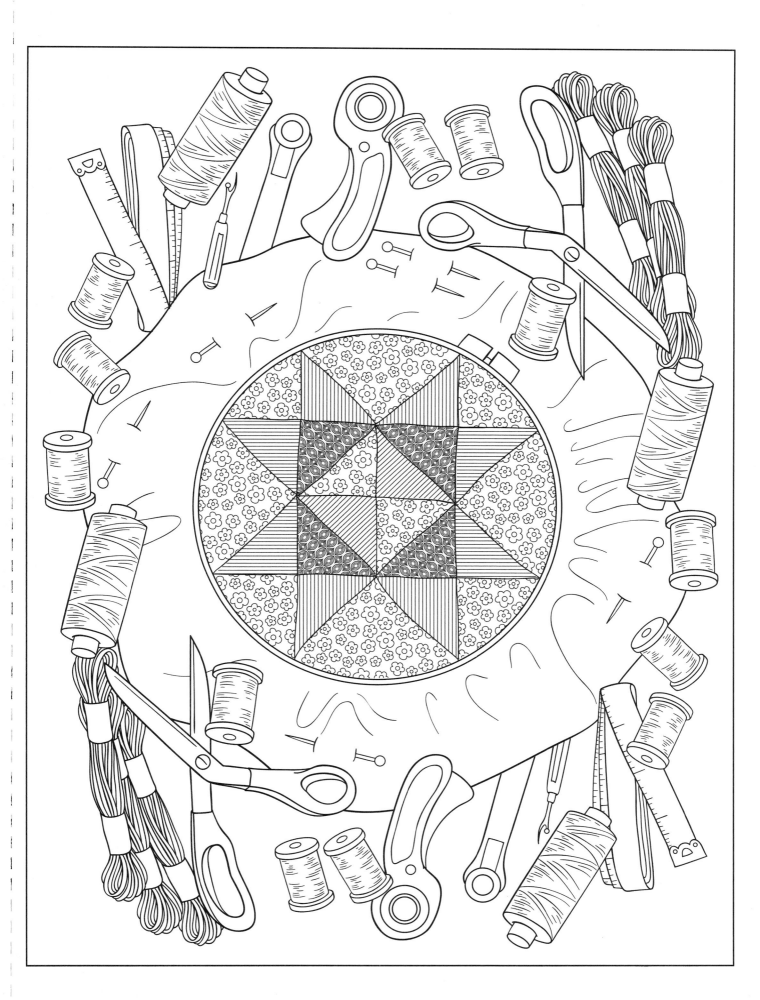

THERE IS NO SUCH *thing as* ENOUGH *Fabric*

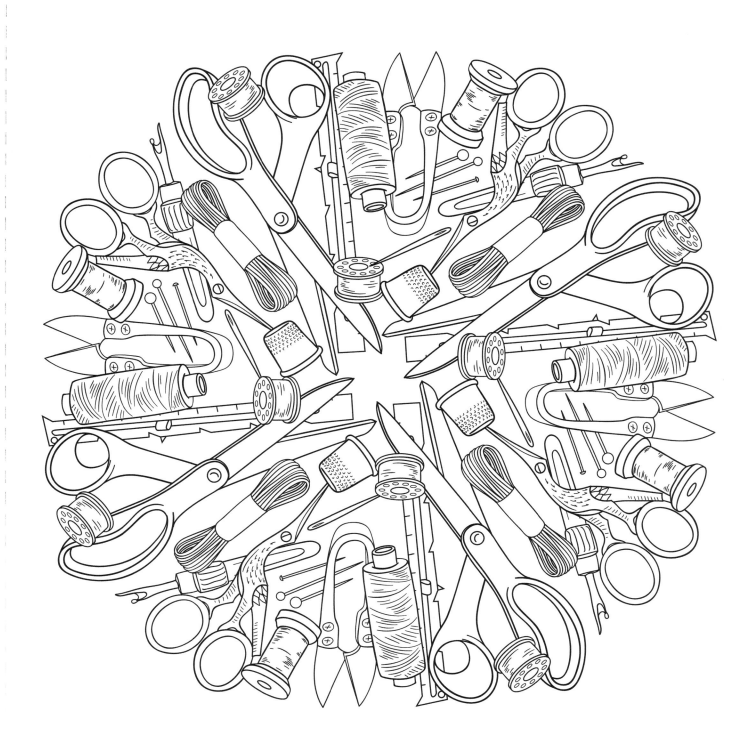

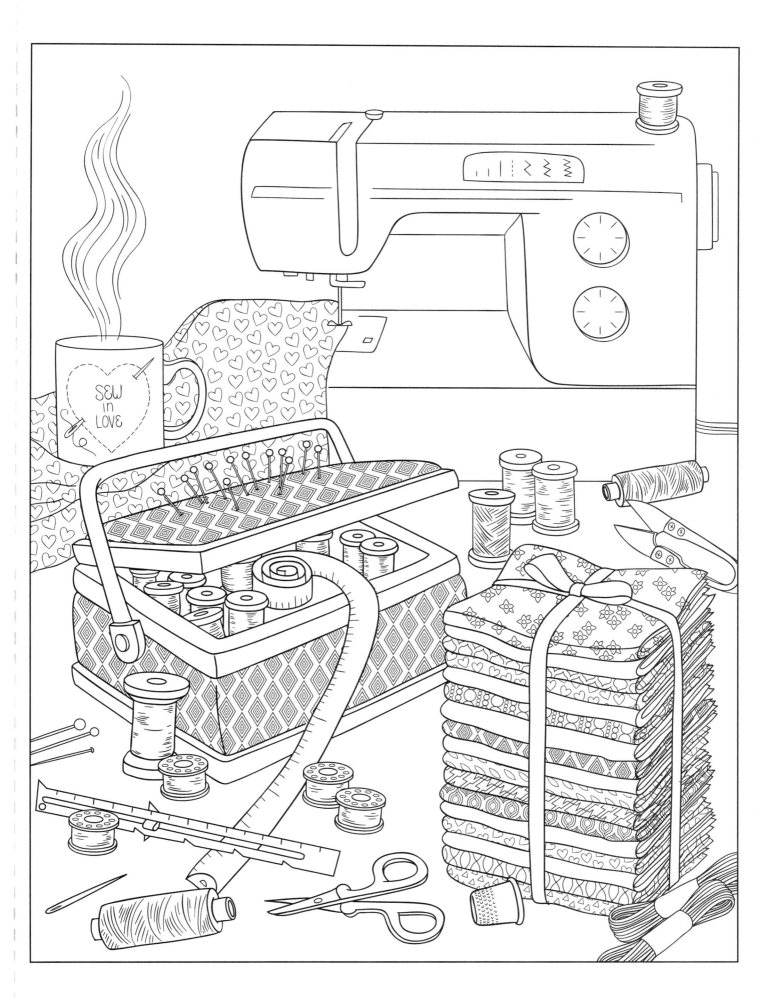

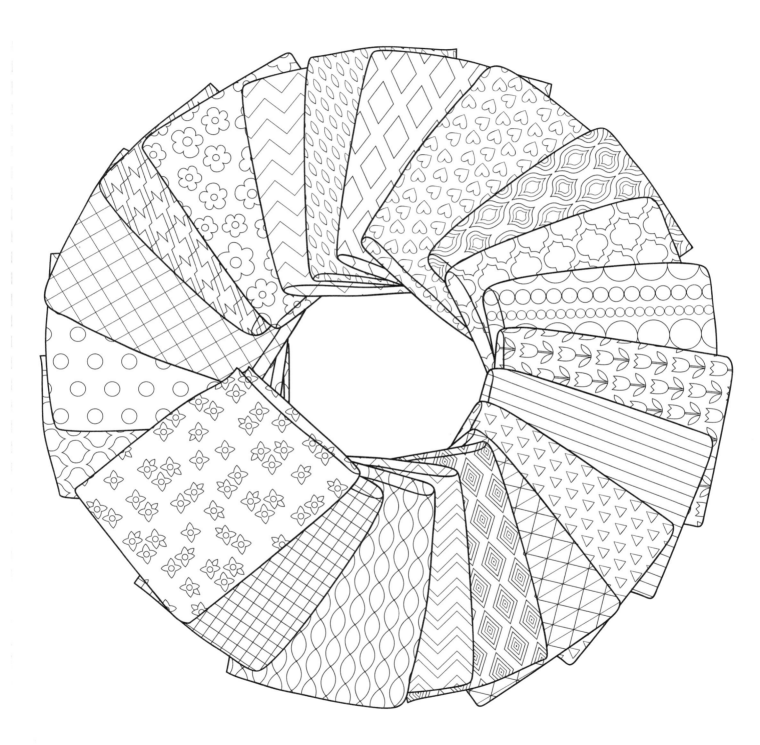

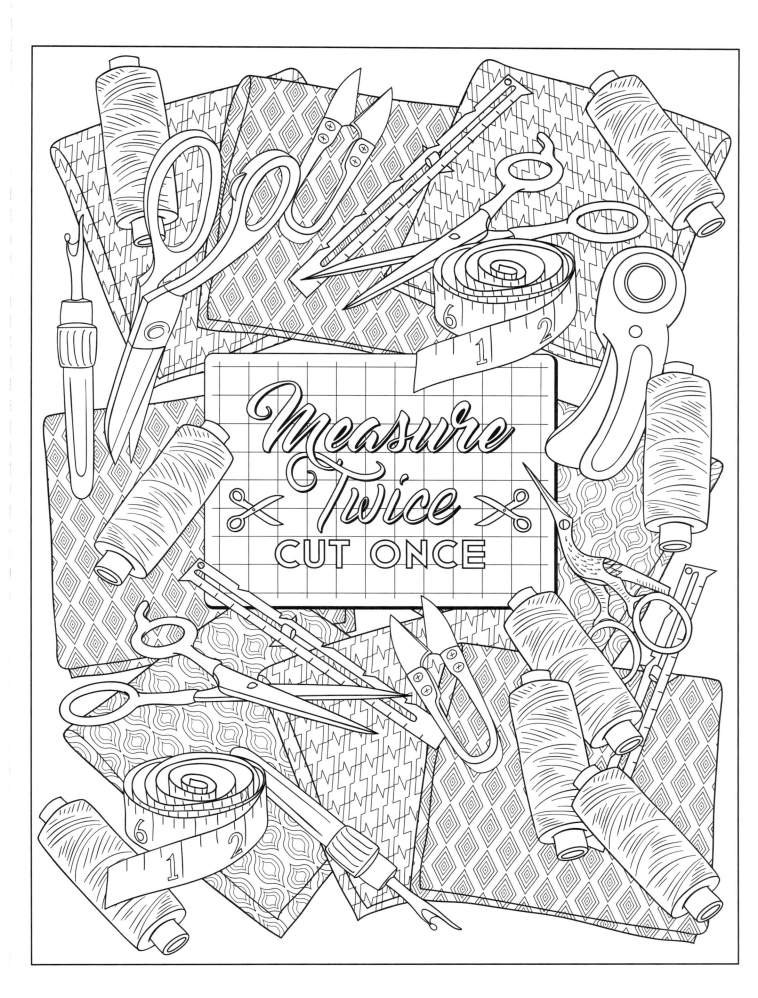

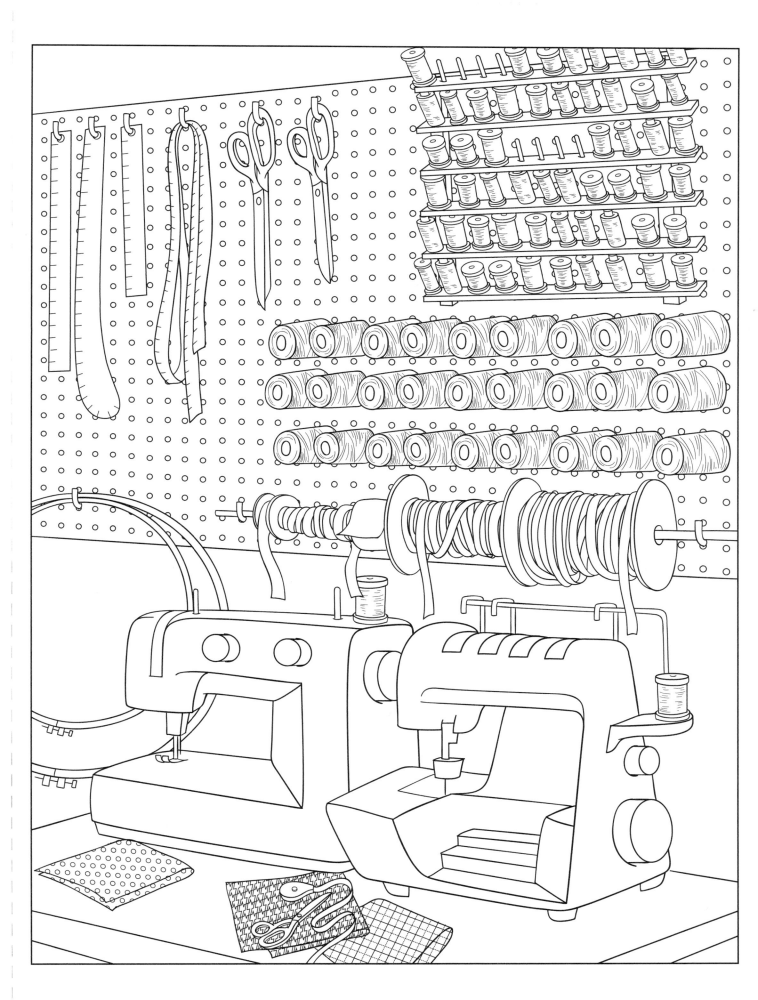